Rookie reader

Thunder
Doesn't
Scare Me!

Written by Lynea Bowdish
Illustrated by John Wallace

Children's Press®
A Division of Grolier Publishing
New York • London • Hong Kong • Sydney
Danbury, Connecticut

For Princess
—L. B.

To Andrew and Leanne
—J. W.

Reading Consultants

Linda Cornwell
Coordinator of School Quality and Professional Improvement
(Indiana State Teachers Association)

Katharine A. Kane
Education Consultant
(Retired, San Diego County Office of Education and San Diego State University)

Visit Children's Press® on the Internet at:
http://publishing.grolier.com

Library of Congress Cataloging-in-Publication Data

Bowdish, Lynea.
  Thunder doesn't scare me! / by Lynea Bowdish ; illustrated by John Wallace.
    p. cm. — (Rookie reader)
  Summary: When thunder makes a young girl and her dog afraid, they decide to
make as much noise as the storm.
  ISBN 0-516-22151-5 (lib. bdg.)   0-516-27291-8 (pbk.)
  [1. Thunderstorms—Fiction. 2. Fear—Fiction. 3. Dogs—Fiction. 4. Noise—Fiction.]
I. Wallace, John, 1966- , ill. II. Title. III. Series.
PZ7.B67194 Tj 2001
[E]—dc21

                    00-038425

GROLIER
PUBLISHING

Princess is afraid of thunder.

But not me.

I help Princess be brave.

Sometimes the thunder goes
BOOM!

We crawl under my bed.

We cover our ears.

13

Sometimes the thunder goes
BOOM! CRACK!

"La, la, la," I sing.
"Ooooooo," Princess howls.

We sound so funny.
We both laugh.

Sometimes the thunder goes
BOOM! CRACK! CRASH!

We have a parade.

I bang my drum.
Princess barks.

We march around the house.

26

I help Princess when it thunders.

We have fun being brave.

Word list (50 words)

a	crack	I	scare
afraid	crash	is	sing
around	crawl	it	so
bang	doesn't	la	sometimes
barks	drum	laugh	sound
be	ears	march	the
bed	fun	me	thunder
being	funny	my	thunders
boom	goes	not	under
both	have	of	we
brave	help	our	when
but	house	parade	
cover	howls	Princess	

About the Author

Princess lives in Hollywood, Maryland, with Chipper and a goldfish. Lynea Bowdish and her husband, David Roberts, live there, too. Princess's absolutely favorite thing, besides dinner and treats, is going for rides with David. She also likes to take naps in the sun on the lounge chair outside. For indoor naps, she has her own small couch in the living room, which Chipper is sometimes allowed to use. Princess's favorite place to sleep is on the king-size bed. When she's feeling energetic, she barks. It's a good life.

About the Illustrator

John Wallace is a full-time author and illustrator of children's books. He works in Brighton, England, where he lives with his wife, Sarah, and his two sons, William and Sam.